LEAFS '65

McClelland & Stewart,

a division of Random House of Canada Limited,

a Penguin Random House Company

www.penguinrandomhouse.ca

1   2   3   4   5   19   18   17   16   15

Penguin
Random
House

WIN A NEW CAR
AT THE PETERBOROUGH MEMORIAL CENTRE
$8,400.00
IN PRIZES
PETERBOROUGH MEMORIAL COMMUNITY CENTRE
SUPERCAR BINGO
FRI SEPT 24
ROCHESTER VS
MAPLE LEAFS SAT
PLYMOUTH

"ARTIST AT LEAFS' CAMP" BY

STEPHEN BRUNT

WITH THE PHOTOGRAPHS OF

LEWIS PARKER

LEAFS '65

THE LOST TORONTO MAPLE LEAFS PHOTOGRAPHS

McClelland & Stewart

"ARTIST AT LEAFS' CAMP"

by STEPHEN BRUNT

One day in 2006, Lewis Parker stood with his friend Dennis Patchett, disposing of some of his past. During his illustrious career as an artist and illustrator, Parker had accumulated boxes and boxes of files and ephemera, some of which now had to go. He and his wife, Eleanor, were moving from their home north of Uxbridge, Ontario into much smaller retirement digs in Toronto. The contents of his studio needed to be sorted, much of it to be given away to other artists, including the boxes of historical research files that had been the basis of some of his best-known work.

That which was deemed not worth saving or bestowing was consigned to a roaring fire in a forty-five-gallon drum. Out in the country, you could still do that kind of thing.

Parker passed the boxes to Patchett, and Patchett pitched them into the inferno, one after another, until a note on a file folder caught his eye: LEAFS 1965. Inside were photographic negatives and contact sheets.

"What are these?" Patchett asked.

Parker began to tell him a story.

"I think we'd better keep them," Patchett said, not yet fully understanding just what it was that he had preserved.

•

Lewis Parker was born in Toronto in 1926 and began studying art at the city's Central Technical School as a thirteen-year-old, leaving three years later to begin work as a junior illustrator with a local firm. He enlisted in the army in 1944, arriving in Europe not long before the Second World War ended. There, as a member of the occupying forces, Parker's artistic talents won him work, first as an illustrator for a regimental newspaper, and later for *The Maple Leaf*, the paper that was distributed to all Canadian servicemen.

Parker returned to Canada in 1946, embarking on a career as a commercial artist. As time went on, he found himself increasingly attracted to historical and aboriginal themes. In 1966, Parker moved with his wife and four children to Mexico, where he studied the Mayans and Aztecs, and then spent time in western Canada, where he learned about the Plains Indians. His first major commission as a historical artist was at the Sainte-Marie Among the Hurons site in Midland, Ontario. He and his painting partner, Gerald Lazare, created the three huge panels inside the dome of the National Museum of Man in Ottawa, a project that took the better part of two years to complete. Next came two large paintings at the restored Fortress of Louisbourg on Cape Breton, depicting the life of the colony in the seventeenth century.

During a career that spanned six decades, Parker established himself as Canada's foremost historic artist, his work famous both for its detailed, painstaking research and for the little slices of humanity that he incorporated into his paintings.

The assignment that produced the lost Leafs pictures was a bit of a career departure.

In the fall of 1965, Parker received a call from *Maclean's* magazine, for which he had done illustrations in the past. They were sending a reporter to Peterborough, Ontario, to cover the Toronto Maple Leafs' preseason training camp. Could he accompany the writer and shoot some stills that could run along with the piece?

It was a conventional job in many ways, but unusual for Parker, who was an excellent photographer as an avocation. He owned a Graflex camera, the standard equipment used by newshounds of the era, but until then had never shot for publication.

On the day the job was to begin, Parker travelled to Toronto's Union Station, where he would catch the train for Peterborough–locals affectionately called it "The Rocket"–in anticipation of spending time with a reporter covering the Leafs. But before boarding, his plans changed. The magazine contacted him to let him know that the reporter had been called away to another assignment. "Go ahead and shoot whatever you want," Parker was told. "When you get back, we'll see if we

can use it." He had three or four days in which to work, and full, unfettered access to the Leafs' camp, including behind the scenes.

Parker shot more than two hundred black-and-white photos during his stay in Peterborough. When he returned to Toronto, he turned the negatives over to the editor at *Maclean's*. The images were both candid and unconventional. It was obvious to anyone who saw them that Parker had brought a different eye to the task than would a news photographer, for whom the job of shooting hockey players was all too ordinary. It's there in the arrangement of the scenes, in the eye for detail, in the unique composition.

A couple of weeks later, Parker got a call from *Maclean's*. The magazine had no use for his pictures. "You might as well keep them," he was told. He filed the negatives away, and there they remained for the next forty-three years, unseen until Dennis Patchett saved them from the fire.

They are published for the first time here.

Training camp was different then.

Today, being a professional hockey player is a twelve-month-a-year proposition. Players may take a little break during the summer months and head for the cottage or travel to more exotic locales, but even then they remain keenly aware of diet and fitness and their conditioning regimens. When they report back to their teams in the fall, most have already been working out and skating on their own. They are tested immediately, and if their cardiopulmonary performance has deteriorated, if their body mass index has skewed even a little bit towards fat, they are told in no uncertain terms that they've failed to live up their obligations—and if they're on the roster bubble, that could be the difference between making the team, a trip to the minors, or the end of the road.

In the early 1960s, when the Parker photographs were taken, there were only six teams in the National Hockey League, the Stanley Cup playoffs were completed in just two best-of-seven rounds, and the trophy was raised in the spring. Players returned to their homes for a long off-season that included rest and relaxation, but often also involved day jobs—even for the stars, hockey salaries weren't the king's ransoms that have since become the norm (Tim Horton, for instance, drove a gravel truck for one of Toronto owner Conn Smythe's companies, and in later years spent the summers tending to his fledgling donut business— including hands-on construction work on at least one of the company's first stores in Hamilton). There was no such thing as summer skating, because there was no such thing as summer ice in arenas. Nor were there formalized workout programs, though it might have seemed as if there were for those who took on physical labour. Most players drank and smoked during the summer months, just as they did during the season. Naturally, they tended to put on a little weight and soften up around the edges.

Training camp was designed to remedy that. It was a time to renew acquaintances, to start thinking about hockey again, and especially to get in shape, which for the Leafs

began with a couple of weeks in Peterborough in September and then continued through six full weeks and fourteen exhibition games before the regular season began. The town, with its strong junior hockey tradition, was a perfect location in many ways—close enough to Toronto that it made for an easy trek back to the Gardens when necessary; far enough away, located as it was on the edges of Ontario's cottage country, that it felt apart from the pressures of the big city, from the distractions of home and family and friends, from the demands of being a Maple Leaf.

Not that there weren't some modest expectations about the condition in which players ought to arrive. Consider the letter sent by the Leafs' coach and general manager, George "Punch" Imlach, to Jim Pappin on August 2, 1962, no doubt almost exactly the same as letters sent to other members of the Toronto Maple Leafs before the 1965 training camp. The one big difference: in 1962, the Leafs were coming off a Stanley Cup victory and were on top of the hockey world; in 1965, they had finished fourth and then lost to Montreal in the first round of the playoffs. Note the line at the end about playoff money. No player was rich enough to take those extra dollars for granted.

Dear Jim:

We will start our Training Camp on Friday, September 7th at Peterboro, Ontario.

All players are to report to the Empress Hotel, Friday morning the 7th. Physical examinations will start at

3

9.00 a.m. through to noon. Dinner will be at 1.00 p.m. After dinner all players will report to the trainers at the arena at 2.30 p.m. and draw their equipment and go for a skate.

Golf will be a must in the Training Camp schedule. Be sure to bring along your golfing equipment. Arrangements have been completed for the use of Kawartha Golf Club during Training Camp.

In view of the fact that nearly all players have cars, I am assuming you will not need railway transportation. However, if you do wish transportation, kindly let us know as soon as possible.

We hope that you have enjoyed the summer and that you will attend Camp with the attitude that now we are Stanley Cup holders we will show everybody that we deserve it and intend to keep it.

I expect you to report in good condition and not more than 7 lbs over your playing weight, with a minimum of being able to do:

20 Push Ups
20 Sit Ups
30 Knee Bends

The competition for jobs on the club should be highly contested this year. We have a good crop of Rookies and they will get every opportunity to make the club. So, let's be ready for the competition and not sorry.

We had a few injuries last year so the better your condition, I believe, the less injuries we will receive.

See you in September and let's make this another profitable year with a big playoff split.

Yours Sincerely,
G. Imlach
General Manager

Imlach was a towering figure in the history of the NHL, though as a player he wasn't particularly special. (A centre with a decent scoring touch, Imlach was on his way when, after a season with the senior Toronto Marlboros, he enlisted in the Canadian Army to serve in the Second World War.) Imlach also coached hockey while in uniform, and would often remark later that his time in the military influenced his thinking and his style. (His players could certainly attest to that that.)

Returning from the service, Imlach was offered a tryout with the Detroit Red Wings, but declined, believing he wasn't really in shape to compete for a big-league job. Instead, he wound up with the Quebec Aces, a senior team, at a time when the calibre of play at that level (and the under-the-table compensation for some star players) wasn't much different than in the NHL. It was in Quebec that Imlach began to develop a career off the ice, first as a player/coach, then as head coach, general manager, and, eventually, part owner of the franchise.

In 1957, Imlach moved to professional hockey, becoming general manager of the Springfield Indians, the top farm club of the Boston Bruins, but was there only a year before ceding control to the returning Eddie Shore at the end of the season.

That July, the Maple Leafs hired the forty-year-old Imlach as an assistant general manager. The team didn't actually have a general manager at the time—the two assistants, Imlach and Francis Michael "King" Clancy, reported to the club's board of directors—but in November 1958, Imlach was promoted into the job. A week after his hiring, he fired coach Billy Reay and added that role to his own duties, for a time employing Bert Olmstead as an assistant player/coach to help out.

Toronto's last Stanley Cup had come way back in 1951—the year Bill Barilko scored the winning goal. By the time Imlach was fired in 1969, his Maple Leaf teams had raised the Cup four times, to date the last golden era in Toronto's long hockey history.

Imlach could be warm and funny when he wanted to. He had an ability to charm the ladies, and especially the sportswriters who followed his team's every move, joking along with them, sharing confidences, playing favourites, and providing plenty of grist for the mill.

But to his players, he was more often a heartless, autocratic, all-powerful boss who loved them when they were winning and abused them when they weren't (sometimes even when they were); who held their destiny, their careers, their paycheques, their futures as professional hockey players, entirely within his hands; who could yell at them, insult them, nail them to the bench, trade them, or exile them to the minors forever,

purely because he felt like it. In other words, he was in every way a man of his time, respected and feared, not unlike the best coaches and managers in other sports, who, thanks to the way the business was structured, were never required to brook dissent or coddle even the biggest stars.

Imlach decided who played for the Maple Leafs (bowing only slightly to the owners), decided how much they were paid, dictated the terms of contracts, and always got his way.

("He was a real queer kind of guy, a bit of a nut," Frank Mahovlich told Douglas Hunter for his book *Open Ice*. "He came out of the army and he kind of ran the team like an army. You can't do that when guys have families. The thing was, the management let him do it, which made them stupid too. It was a terrible, terrible situation.")

By the time the Maple Leafs and their various farm teams gathered for training camp in the fall of 1965, signs were popping up all around that a revolution was brewing in professional sport—though, in the moment, few would have connected the dots—and that figures like Imlach were slowly but surely heading towards extinction.

Big-league hockey had remained fundamentally unchanged since 1942, when the NHL settled into its familiar six-team configuration—the so-called Original Six. The players, nearly all of them Canadian, were products of a system that required them to sign over the rights to their professional services to one of those clubs as teenagers, effectively in perpetuity. Players were paid what the owners, general managers, and coaches dictated. Rock the boat, and they'd be banished to one of the league's lesser franchises or, more likely, to the distant minor leagues, where many an NHL-calibre talent toiled in obscurity, for peanuts. To even dare discuss forming a union—as a small, brave band led by Ted Lindsay had done during the late 1950s—entailed the risk of being declared a dangerous, disposable subversive, no matter how great one's ability.

By the fall of 1965, cracks were starting to appear in the old power structure. Plans were underway for the NHL to undertake the most ambitious expansion in the history of professional sport, doubling in size from six to twelve franchises all at once in the 1967–68 season, and taking the northern game into exotic southern climes in the United States. For the owners, the lure was money, of course, from fees that could be collected from the owners of the new teams and from an expected bonanza in American network television dollars once the league had established a footprint extending all the way to California.

For the players, expansion represented something else: liberation. In one fell swoop, the number of big-league professional hockey jobs would double. Players now riding the buses in the American, Central, or Western leagues would be in high demand. Those who had hit a dead end in Toronto or Montreal or Detroit, who had been held back because a coach didn't like them or because there was a logjam of talent at their position, would suddenly find their paths to the NHL clear—and perhaps have a chance to live among the beaches and palm trees as a bonus.

That new, far more open market for players would also be stoked by other developments behind the scenes.

Had any of the 1965 Maple Leafs walked into Imlach's office to negotiate a contract and brought along a lawyer, an accountant, or even a buddy who understood numbers a little better than they did, they'd have been thrown out immediately and told to come back, alone, after they'd regained their senses.

Just a year later, a brilliant young defenceman from Parry Sound, Ontario, named Bobby Orr, who had signed away his rights to the Boston Bruins when he was fourteen years old, hired a lawyer, Alan Eagleson, to negotiate his first contract. The Bruins balked—at first. But Orr was a talent for the ages, and the sad-sack franchise was desperate for a saviour, so Eagleson was allowed to demand a deal that made the rookie the highest-paid player in the league. The genie was out of the bottle. Other players obviously didn't enjoy nearly the same degree of leverage, but soon enough they would almost all be employing lawyers or player agents to negotiate on their behalf. And eventually, they would also be supported by a union, formed under Eagleson's leadership in 1966. What was coming, inevitably, though in some sports more quickly than others, was true free agency, allowing the same athletes previously bound by C Forms and reserve clauses to sell their services on the open market to the highest bidder once their contracts had expired.

In 1965, that day still lay beyond the horizon. In the meantime, players who were attempting to negotiate better contracts, understanding that they couldn't sell their services to another team, had but one risky option: to withhold their services. Joe DiMaggio of the New York Yankees did it, way back in the 1930s, and during the spring of 1966, two of the most famous players in baseball, Sandy Koufax and Don Drysdale, the all-star foundation of the Los Angeles Dodgers' pitching rotation, would hold out together in an attempt to force the team's ownership to give them lucrative multiyear deals. That same year, the previously toothless Major League Baseball Players Association hired a former United Steelworkers negotiator named Marvin Miller as its head, and the notion of what a sports union could be was forever changed.

In hockey in the fall of 1965, the only real call to arms was coming from the biggest star in the game, Bobby Hull of the Chicago Black Hawks, who was loudly demanding to be paid the princely sum of $100,000 a season. It was time, Hull said, for the players to start working together and sharing information in order to improve their lot.

"Some players are better at negotiating than others," he said. "If knowing what other players are being paid helps him, a player has the right to know. The players all grumble about their salaries but they won't stick together and do something about it. Some of them are afraid to be holdouts in case they're sent to the minors."

All of that was background noise as the Maple Leafs opened camp in Peterborough. In the foreground, there were more immediate concerns, a myriad of issues and stories surrounding a team that was coming off a disappointing season.

During a pre-camp press luncheon at the Hot Stove Lounge at Maple Leaf Gardens, Imlach, Toronto Marlboros general manager Jim Gregory, and Ray Miron, who ran the Leafs' Central Hockey League affiliate in Tulsa, went through the list of concerns and issues heading into the new season.

Ron Ellis was recovering from midsummer knee surgery, following a terrific rookie campaign in 1964–65 during which he had scored twenty-three goals.

"We expect him to be ready for the start of the National Hockey League season," Imlach said of the twenty-year-old right winger. "He's got a lot of time."

At the other end of the spectrum, Imlach confirmed that Dickie Moore, who had attempted a comeback the previous season with discouraging results, wouldn't be back for another year.

"He's told us he's through," Imlach said (though Moore would in fact return for a swan-song season with the expansion St. Louis Blues in 1967).

The coach acknowledged that right wing, behind Ellis and Jim Pappin, might be a trouble spot and that he might consider moving defenceman Tim Horton there, as he had when injuries thinned the roster during the previous season. Horton had responded by scoring eight goals, but everything being equal, Imlach still preferred to leave him on defence.

George Armstrong, the Leafs' captain, wasn't guaranteed a starting spot unless he picked up his game after a rough year. Mike Walton, a former junior star who had been the rookie of the year the previous season in the Central league, had a shot to make the big team, but centre was the team's deepest position, so he'd be competing against Dave Keon, Bob Pulford, Pete Stemkowski, Eddie Joyal, and tough guy Orland Kurtenbach, who had come over from the Bruins in a trade for Ron Stewart. It was hard to like Walton's chances.

The Leafs had lost two goaltenders in the intra-league draft: Don Simmons to the New York Rangers and Gerry Cheevers to the Boston Bruins. But Imlach wasn't concerned, even though his two holdovers were awfully long in the tooth.

"The odds against Johnny Bower and Terry Sawchuk going over the hill together, or being hurt at the same time, are so great I don't even think about it," Imlach said.

(Imlach, though he loved his elderly goalies, was also planning ahead in a way that seems visionary in retrospect. That fall, he had tried and failed to persuade the Czechoslovakian ice hockey federation to allow a twenty-three-year-old goaltender named Vladimir Dzurilla to come to North America and sign with the Leafs. The Czech authorities refused—it would be years before any players arrived in the NHL from behind the former Iron Curtain—and so Dzurilla returned to his club team in Bratislava. But Canadian hockey fans of a certain age remember him well: he was the roly-poly netminder who shut out what might have been the best Team Canada ever assembled, 1–0, in a game at the Montreal Forum during the round-robin portion of the 1976 Canada Cup. Canada came back and won that tournament—the Czechoslovakians took the silver—and Dzurilla played on until 1982, representing his country in three Olympics and a host of world championships.)

The fact was, Bower was forty-one. Sawchuk was thirty-six. Allan Stanley was thirty-nine, Red Kelly thirty-eight, Marcel Pronovost and Horton both thirty-five. This was an ancient group.

No worries, the coach said. As far as Imlach was concerned, thirty-five represented the prime of life for a hockey player.

There were a bunch of new arrivals with the squad, the result of a couple of big trades during the off-season. In May, the Leafs had sent Andy Bathgate, Billy Harris, and Gary Jarrett to the Detroit Red Wings in return for Autry Erickson, Larry Jeffrey, Eddie Joyal, Lowell MacDonald, and Pronovost. In June, they'd dealt Ron Stewart to Boston in return for Kurtenbach, Andy Hebenton, and a young defenceman named Pat Stapleton—whom they would immediately lose to the Chicago Black Hawks in the intra-league draft.

Of all the incoming players, Pronovost, still one of the league's best defencemen, was expected to have the most impact, while Kurtenbach would add some grit.

On the good-news front, at least from the Leafs' point of view, versatile veteran Leonard "Red" Kelly had decided to give up his second career as a member of Parliament and focus entirely on hockey. The strain of the twin responsibilities had proven too much for him and his family.

"The travelling wasn't the worst part of it, either," Kelly said. "I think the toughest thing to accept was that you were never away from the job—not for one second."

Frank Mahovlich, the most gifted player on the Leafs' squad, was returning fresh from a two-and-a-half-month trip to Europe with his wife, taken in hopes of escaping the pressure of hockey in Toronto following a season in which he was forced to leave the team after suffering a nervous breakdown. As far as anyone could tell, he arrived in Peterborough refreshed and in good spirits.

A familiar last name was on the training camp roster: Brian Conacher, son of Lionel, nephew of Charlie, was trying out for the team and debating whether to leave university and surrender his amateur status and his spot on Canada's national team.

"I'm confident I have the ability to play in the National league with the Leafs or I wouldn't be here," Conacher said. "I don't think I have to stick around for a month and play twenty exhibition games to prove I belong. Not that I have anything against a month of training camp, but I don't want to miss too much school if that's where I'm going to wind up. . . . I want a two-year contract and the money has to be right. Under certain conditions, I might go to the minors if they felt I needed more seasoning."

Eddie Shack, a fan favourite in Toronto, was in camp but already ticketed for the Rochester Americans of the American Hockey League, the Leafs' top minor-league affiliate. The theory was that he'd sell tickets there—a prospect particularly appealing to Imlach, who was a silent partner in ownership of the Rochester team. Shack wasn't happy about it, but it was unlikely he'd change Imlach's mind, especially since his undisciplined play had put him permanently in the coach's doghouse.

"To everyone's surprise, Eddie Shack showed up at camp in peak form," columnist Red Burnett wrote in the *Toronto Star*. "Fast Eddie bypassed Imlach and greeted Rochester manager-coach Joe Crozier with enthusiasm. Rumours had it that Shack would delay his arrival at camp to protest his official demotion to Rochester."

There were also other small pieces of business. Lowell MacDonald needed a tonsillectomy, and so was absent for the time being. Larry Keenan was coming off knee surgery.

"Barrie Ross, drafted from St. Paul for $10,000, has informed Leafs he intends to stick to his barbering business in Yorkton, Saskatchewan," Burnett wrote.

Early in camp, the Leafs picked up another goaltender, acquiring the rights to Bruce Gamble from the Boston Bruins. Gamble had spent the previous eighteen months back home in Fort William, Ontario, because it was preferable to playing for the tyrannical Eddie Shore, who ran the Bruins' top farm club in Springfield.

Meanwhile, one of Toronto's incumbent goalies was dealing with a pressing issue of his own. Sawchuk was trying to find a four-bedroom house for rent in Toronto where his family could stay, and he put out the word through the newspapermen, hoping that someone among their readership might know of a place that would work. In the meantime, he ducked out after medicals to attend a wedding.

It wasn't just the Leafs who were training in Peterborough. The organization's minor-league affiliates from Rochester and Tulsa were there as well, with players occasionally being shuttled back and forth from the big team, depending on how they were performing and whether or not they were in Imlach's good graces. The Peterborough Memorial Arena was a crowded place, with storerooms pressed into service as temporary dressing rooms for minor leaguers.

Among the players housed there was a thirty-one-year-old journeyman minor-league defenceman bound for Tulsa with just a single NHL game to his credit: Don Cherry.

The biggest news coming out of Peterborough was the fact that a group of players were still unsigned to contracts for the coming season, including the heart of the Leafs' defensive corps—Horton, Bob Baun, and Carl Brewer—and forwards Pulford, Keon, and Kelly.

But really, that wasn't so unusual for the Leafs, or for any NHL team of the era. At some point during camp, the unsigned players would individually file into Imlach's office, haggle with him as best they could, extract some modest concessions or a minimal raise, and then sign on the dotted line. It wasn't as if they had much choice or could exert any real leverage. The bottom line was they could either play for the Leafs for what the club was willing to pay them, or not play at all.

Imlach certainly wasn't above negotiating through the press, turning on the sarcasm and casting his players as greedy ingrates, especially given the disappointing results of the previous season. You can be sure that most of the fans at home reading the newspapers thought exactly the same way. It's a kid's game, after all. And it's the beloved Maple Leafs. Who hadn't dreamed of wearing that uniform? Who wouldn't love to play hockey for a living?

"You should hear my guys," Imlach told a group of reporters. "They say they're the best. You'd have thought we won the league and the Stanley Cup instead of finishing out in the first round last season. All of them had great years. I can't figure out how we lost if they all played that well."

Imlach's boss, Stafford Smythe, stood supportively behind his coach and general manager.

"I guess Punch still has the holdout committee to deal with," he said. "It's the same every year. I'd like to make them sign bonus contracts which would get them what they want, but only if they produce what we expect."

Just when the holdouts would sign was one of many questions to be answered over the next six weeks by a team that seemed no more likely to mount a serious challenge for the Stanley Cup than it had the season before, that appeared to be aging and in decline, a shadow of the squads that were winning championships at the beginning of the decade.

"The next six weeks and 14 exhibition games provide the most interesting camp Leafs have held in a half dozen years," reporter Ken McKee wrote.

Truth is, he didn't know the half of it.

Soon after arriving in Peterborough, the hockey beat reporters and columnists sat with Imlach in the stands and duly recorded his thoughts as one of the first training camp practices played out. This is how Dick Beddoes described the scene in his *Globe and Mail* column, published on September 21, 1965:

This is the hockey camp of the Toronto Maple Leafs, as seen any morning or afternoon from the top row of seats in Peterborough's Memorial Centre.

Down on a grey rectangle of chipped ice, ambitious athletes in a gay assortment of coloured jerseys are skating, shooting, wheezing and seating.

The sounds are purely physical—the harsh slam of one man draping another on the boards, the heavy whunk of a puck driven against a goaltender's pads, the quick, coarse scrape of skates on ice.

And up in the top row, the unceasing editorial comment out of George Imlach, the presiding steward.

When Frank Mahovlich leaps across a blue line, slaps the puck between John Bower and the goal post, and Bower makes one cat move to stop the puck: "Anybody but Bower and that's a goal—and I mean anybody!"

When Tim Horton, guarding the blue line, jolts young men named Bob Kilger and Andre Hinse with full, erect

body-checks and they fall, winded: "That's the way to knock a man loose from his toenails! Murder Incorporated!"

For five days this has been going on, 69 players scrambling for assignments to the Leafs, to Rochester or Victoria, hoping to escape relegation to the lower hockey burgs. Indolently wanting, a spectator could see a few signs and tell himself that they might be significant.

A guy could see Mahovlich skating in his wild-horse-on-the-goose style and tell himself that this is what the game is all about, the great strides of a superb skater overpowering the enemy defence.

But Imlach is containing his enthusiasm for Mahovlich on the move, hoping this prodigy with the puck will stay fit and enthusiastic for a full season.

Last winter, Mahovlich came unstrung emotionally and missed five weeks of the season. By the time he returned, the Leafs were sagging, objects of scorn and abuse in the Gardens.

This summer, Mahovlich and his wife toured Europe for 10 weeks, away from the pressures of hockey's small, tight world. He came back spiritually refreshed, apparently recharged to meet the demands of his psyche and talent.

A fellow could witness Red Kelly, the retired member of Parliament, a blue turtleneck vest protecting his throat, a small, round part in his red haircut. He seems less preoccupied than at any time since he became burdened with a political briefcase.

Kelly was bored by the foot-dragging of Parliament, but his reason for quitting the Liberals still stands. He wanted more time with his wife and three little income-tax deductions.

So how did his wife feel when he decided to abandon a parliamentary career?

"I think she was relieved," Kelly said, thoughtfully, "she broke down and cried . . ."

Now Horton could be heard swatting people again, as though he was relieving two recent irritations. Timothy is in the hamburger game in Toronto, the proprietor of several meat-patty palaces. Not long ago, a disgruntled customer exploded a bomb in the washroom of one of Horton's drive-in restaurants.

"That seems like pretty loud criticism of the food," Horton mused as he cleaned up the debris.

Then, last weekend, thieves stole his new car from outside the Horton household. Police found it Sunday, banged up like a tin can that has been molested by a pile driver.

Horton did the deadpan bit. "I think the customers are trying to tell me something. I guess I better sell the hamburger stands . . ."

Here was lively action around Bower, and here came the puck, driven fast and accurately, knee-high. In the smallest fraction of a second, the old gentleman kicked up his bulky pad and deflected the shot.

"Ho, boy!" Mr. Imlach chortled. "What a lovely old burglar he is!"

Bower is rising 41, but he is exhibiting the double sharpness of a two-edged razor. That's okay with most of us. As long as Bower can stick in the NHL, we've got a link with an era when we were all a lot younger.

•

Reporters also enjoyed an audience with King Clancy, Imlach's assistant, an impish Irishman who had been a great hockey player in his day, and who would serve as the good cop to Imlach's bad cop—just as, years later, he would play the genial sidekick during the dark era when the team was owned by Harold Ballard.

Clancy remembered what a Maple Leafs training camp was like in the old days. His first was in 1930, in Parry Sound, where Conn Smythe brought twelve of his players to chop wood, exercise, take long walks, and sweat off their summer fat. By comparison, he said, this was a vacation for the players, and an expensive one. The club's training camp budget had soared to almost $40,000.

But even as he pined for those simpler, tougher days, Clancy said he liked the look of this group of modern Leafs, especially after some of the changes made during the off-season.

"We've got rid of the feather dusters and replaced them with brawn and muscle," he said. "I've been in over thirty hockey camps, as player, coach and what have you, and I've never seen so many big guys on the ice at one time with one team. What meat and muscle—and most of them can skate. There's bound to be action when Orland Kurtenbach and Larry Jeffrey and those young giants from our farm teams start flexing their muscles. I can hardly wait to see someone make the mistake of taking a reef at Pronovost or Kurtenbach. And it's bound to happen."

•

Just three days into camp, Brian Conacher walked out, declaring his intention to remain an amateur and enroll at the University of Western Ontario.

With his uncle Charlie, the former Leaf great, quietly advising him in the background, Conacher had asked Imlach for a two-year, no-cut contract, with a $7,500 signing bonus and a $15,000 salary the first season, $17,500 the second.

Imlach's response, as reported by Conacher in his biography: "No ——ing. . . . way."

When asked to explain Conacher's departure from camp, Imlach didn't mince words.

"Not only did he want a good chunk of dough, but he also wanted me to make a decision, now, on whether he'd be kept with the big squad.

"I'd have been stupid to have told Conacher he was on the Leafs after only four days of training camp. He can't make the difference on whether I'll win the Stanley Cup or not. The guys that will win it for me are like Ellis and Keon and Mahovlich and the goaltenders.

"Conacher showed well here, but how could I pick him ahead of the guys I've got on left wing? There's no way I can say that he's better than Mahovlich, Jeffrey, Selby and maybe Pulford or Kelly, whom I might switch over there. . . .

"I told him he had a good future in hockey if he wants to use it. Expansion is coming up and when there are six more big league teams, there'll be twice as many jobs. But if I had assured him of a job on the Leafs now, it would have been unfair to the rest of the team. . . . Nobody comes in and becomes the president of the bank right away. He's got to empty some wastebaskets first."

Conacher moved to London, began the university term, and waited—and waited—for Imlach to capitulate. The phone call never came. His uncle Charlie advised him not to make the first move, to remain patient, but after a week he couldn't take it any longer. Conacher called Imlach and said he was prepared to go the minors for a year if necessary. From there, things fell into place: $35,000 for two years, a number that stayed the same whether Conacher was with the Leafs or with Rochester or Tulsa (in modern hockey parlance, a "one-way" contract), the most Imlach had ever paid a rookie.

"Conacher can be sent anywhere in the Leaf chain," Imlach explained. "Where he ends up depends on how good he is on the ice. We think he has a chance to make the big team. And he signed for much the same contract we offered him earlier."

"The fact that I'm a Conacher helped me work out a better contract and get my foot inside professional hockey's door," Conacher said. "But no one knows better than I that from here on, I'm on my own. Uncle Charlie laid the cards on the table when we discussed my becoming a Leaf and my chances of success in the NHL. He made it clear that once I hit the ice, I'm on my own, that the fact that I am a Conacher will make them check me that much tighter and that I'll have to work that much harder. I have no illusions about this being a soft touch and I know that I'm green as a professional. If I have to go to Rochester or Tulsa to improve my play, I'll go."

·

There were other young players in camp, all of whom faced daunting odds to make the team. Even the bluest of blue-chip prospects had two truths working against them.

In a six-team league, only a tiny handful of first-year players managed to displace veterans from lineups, and many of those had spent multiple seasons in the minors before finally making the breakthrough. Most seasons, there were at most a dozen players eligible for consideration as the NHL's rookie of the year.

And in Toronto, there was the added complication of Imlach's oft-stated preference for veteran players. All things being equal, Imlach would choose an old warhorse over a bright young prospect every time, though a truly remarkable talent could sway his opinion. The season before, Ron Ellis had made the jump straight from the junior Marlboros to the Leafs, and two other Leafs during the Imlach era had claimed the Calder Memorial Trophy: Dave Keon in 1960–61 and Kent Douglas in 1962–63—though Douglas was in fact a twenty-six-year-old minor-pro veteran the year he was named the NHL's best rookie.

In 1965, the two young players most likely to crack the Leafs' lineup were Brit Selby and Mike Walton.

Selby, a high-scoring winger with the Marlboros team that won the Memorial Cup in 1964—he put eighty-eight points on the board in fifty-two games in his last junior season—had already enjoyed a brief taste of the NHL,

filling in for the injured Ellis with the Leafs for three games, scoring two goals.

Walton, from Kirkland Lake, Ontario, was also on that Memorial Cup squad along with Ellis, Jim McKenny, Pete Stemkowski, and Gary Smith. He followed that up with an excellent first season in professional hockey, when he was named the Central Hockey League's rookie of the year while playing for the Toronto farm team in Tulsa, and also made the CHL's first all-star team.

Walton had inherited the nickname "Shakey" from his father, a hockey player who enjoyed a long career in the senior and minor professional ranks, including winning an Allan Cup, a stint with the Wembley Lions in England, and a four-game call-up with the Montreal Canadiens during the Second World War. The younger Walton was more of a true talent than his old man, but in Imlach's book, he had a couple of strikes against him: he was one of the first Leafs to try and push the boundaries of personal style, wearing long hair and sideburns in what forever had been a crew-cut game; and he dated, and eventually married, the niece of owner Stafford Smythe, which the coach didn't like at all.

Though he would eventually earn a reputation for flamboyance, for 1960s-style rebellion—and, like Mahovlich and Ellis, would battle depression—the Walton who spoke with a reporter in September 1965 sounded just like any other hopeful rookie, albeit one who, thanks to his father's less-than-glamorous career, had a slightly different outlook on the business of the game.

"It's an ambition I had since I was a kid in Fort William . . . to play in the National League. Now, maybe . . . ," Walton said. "I think I'll make the Leafs eventually, but this is the year I want to. I want to stay up, now. . . .

"Hockey players were looked on a little as bums in my dad's time, but today the game's got a high-class tone."

The next episode of high drama at Leafs training camp originated from a predictable source.

Eddie Shack was a unique hockey player and a unique human being, a former butcher from Sudbury, Ontario, who was so prone to wandering all over the ice, it was hard to know which position he was playing. The fans loved him, loved his hyperaggressive style, loved his slightly goofy nature. His nickname was "The Entertainer," with good reason.

But his coach wasn't nearly so entertained or enamoured.

"He's not going to be a member of this team," Imlach said early in camp, announcing that Shack had been demoted to the Rochester Americans and would play the season there. "We could afford him when the team was winning. But he scored only five goals last year. We have to replace him with somebody.

"He got plenty of cheers from the fans, but that bothered some of the other players. They felt if Shack was going to get all the credit, he could do the work. It was a situation we had to correct."

It was entirely within Imlach's powers to make the call, and Shack could be left in Rochester for a whole season before the Leafs would have to expose him to waivers. But Shack balked and refused to sign his contract. Pencilled in to play for Rochester against the Leafs in an exhibition game staged to benefit a charity for disabled children, he refused to go on the ice.

He was immediately suspended and ordered by Americans coach Joe Crozier to check out of the Empress Hotel. While training camp continued without him, Shack spent a day with his family in Peterborough and thought things over.

"Of course I'm upset about how they're treating me," he said. "Imlach hasn't said two words to me in this camp. If he doesn't want me, he should deal me to Boston or Detroit, because I hear they both want me. He at least ought to give me a chance to stay in the NHL instead of sending me to the minors for box office reasons."

Everyone had figured that part out. The Americans were going to be playing ten of their home games the following spring at Maple Leaf Gardens because their home rink was going to be occupied by a bowling tournament. Imlach wanted Shack with the Amerks to help sell tickets.

The exhibition game went on, the crowd in Peterborough chanted, "We want Shack," and Imlach remained unmoved.

"If you're going to walk out, you don't do it in a game being played for charity," he said.

But before he could send a notice of suspension to the NHL head office, Shack had second thoughts, returned to camp contrite, and dutifully signed his contract—a "two-way" deal, which meant he'd be paid less in the American league than if he played for the Leafs.

"I'm glad Eddie got straightened out," Imlach said. "He has been treated the way I would treat any other player in camp. This type of thing helps no one. Actually. It was a lot of fuss over nothing."

Shack complained that he could make as much money selling cars as he could playing for Rochester. It was only the faint chance of returning to the Leafs or being dealt to another NHL team that convinced him to sign, he explained.

"I'm hoping I can play well enough to get back with the big team or make it possible for them to make a good deal for me," Shack said. "I still haven't changed my mind regarding my ability to play in the National Hockey League. . . . I was mad, upset and confused (when I walked out). Let's face it, playing hockey is a nice way to make your living. Now all I want to do is forget all the rumpus and the things that have been said and written over the past couple of days. Starting today, I'm going to concentrate on hockey and try to play my way back into the NHL."

On September 25, 1965, Ted Galambos of the *Peterborough Examiner* wrote a story that in the moment wouldn't have seemed out of the ordinary, but that by the end of camp would resonate in an entirely unexpected way. It was a profile of Leafs defenceman Carl Brewer that ran under the headline "A visit with a

professional athlete—Rewards in a hockey player's life are worth the bumps and bruises."

Brewer was coming off what was arguably the best season of his professional career, after which he was named to the NHL's second all-star team—which meant he was considered one of the best four defencemen in hockey. He was a bright guy who was pursuing a university education while playing, different enough from most of his confreres to be considered a bit of an eccentric. But nothing in the story, which also paints a pretty good picture of the daily routine of training camp, suggests what would happen just days after its publication.

Hockey has been Carl Brewer's life for 17 years and it has been good to him.

The eight-year veteran defenceman for the Toronto Maple Leafs wouldn't trade professional hockey for anything else.

The 27-year-old Toronto native first started playing organized hockey on a peewee hockey team. He moved on through the Toronto minor hockey system into Junior B competition and finally played with the Toronto Marlboros of the OHA Junior A league.

Brewer joined the Maple Leafs in the 1958–59 season and is one of several Toronto players who jumped from Junior A hockey into professional ranks without going to some other minor league.

"Hockey is a good way of life," said Brewer. "I have been very fortunate. You have to be because only one out of 120 make the NHL each year. If I had my life to live

over, there is very little that I would like to change. I have enjoyed playing in the NHL for seven years."

For the last eight days, Brewer has been one of the more than 70 players attending the Maple Leafs' training camp in Peterborough.

Every day since training started September 18, Brewer's thoughts have been on hockey. The day starts at 6:15 a.m. and it may not end until 11:15 p.m.–sometimes earlier. In those 17 hours or less, Brewer will have gone through a couple of hockey practices, a game of golf and an evening of relaxation before lights out at 11:15 p.m. at the Empress Hotel.

Many a night, Brewer, like most of the Maple Leaf players, are in bed and asleep hours before "lights out" as they are mentally and physically tired.

Early on the morning of Sept. 16, Brewer left his wife and daughter in Toronto and drove to Peterborough. He won't see his family again until Oct. 3, when the Maple Leafs play an exhibition game at Maple Leaf Gardens against the New York Rangers.

Brewer checked into the hotel and went through his medical checkup before noon. In the afternoon, he joined the other players in a light skate at the Memorial Centre. There was another skating session after supper.

Then to bed until a call from the hotel desk at 6:15 a.m.

"We have breakfast and there is a great quantity of food," said Brewer. "We have juice, eggs, toast, bacon, cereal, milk, jam and coffee. For the players who have to watch their weight there is a good training table.

"After breakfast all the players walk to the rink. This helps us digest the meal. We are then on the ice for an hour and a half. We have scrimmages and more scrimmages. When the practice is over, you are pretty tired.

"After this practice we play golf. Some play nine holes, others play 18. I really enjoy walking, although I don't play too well. The hills at the Kawartha are good for the conditioning and the air feels good.

"The evenings are left up to the individual. Sometimes there are meetings. Some of the players go to movies or just sit in their rooms and talk or read.

"I am usually pretty tired by night and I take a good hot bath and read. The aches and pains come through by then."

Brewer, a quiet-spoken and well-dressed young athlete, doesn't feel that a training camp is a grind, but he said it depends on the individual. "Once you get your legs and your wind and your stamina, it becomes less of a grind. The first week here is darn tough."

He said he would rather train in Peterborough than in Toronto. A training camp is good because it gets the players together in new surroundings and builds up spirit.

Brewer said in Peterborough the players have a chance to communicate with each other after a day of practice. They can talk about missed passes and goals scored. If the players trained in Toronto, those who live in Toronto would go home after a workout, while the others would be grouped together in a hotel.

"All the players like to train here. They like the town, the rink and the good ice. It is a pleasant town in which to get away from the telephone calls at home.

"I am in good shape, but conditioning is a state of

mind. Just before camp opens, I start to run a great deal. My thoughts are never free from hockey. I always have the view that next year will be my year. You train all the time."

Brewer is a few subjects away from receiving a bachelor of arts degree. He takes correspondence courses during the winter months and has spent some summers at university.

He is one of those players who doesn't have to watch their weight closely during the off-season. He said he doesn't take on any special summer training program to keep his weight near the 180 pounds which he has during the hockey campaign.

This past summer, he worked around the house and didn't vary more than two or three pounds from his playing weight. He could put on the weight after a couple of meals.

"This year I worked out three or four days before training camp opened. I ran, did some physical exercises, played some basketball and football. Physical activity is good for a person."

The mental attitude toward getting ready for a training camp is important. A person could be in good physical shape, but "conditioning is still a state of mind."

As a defenceman, Brewer has to do a great amount of skating in a game. He has to go ahead, skate backwards, stop and go more often than forwards.

"Physical training is good. I enjoy exercising. However, skating drills are tedious, but many good things in life are tedious. Hockey is your life, so you have to do these exercises to strengthen your skating.

"A player's legs are his bread and butter. Strong arms are a necessity, so you do some exercises for them, too. A players also needs good stomach muscles, as these affect everything he does in a game."

Brewer, who "gets along" with the other members of the Maple Leafs, has been coached by only two people—Walter (Turk) Broda when he was with the Marlies, and George (Punch) Imlach, the Leafs' coach and general manager.

"Both coaches are about the same as far as conditioning is concerned. Broda was a tough man. He was going all out all the time. Imlach is much the same. As a junior team, we really skated and we tried to work on our weaknesses."

Bob Haggert, Toronto's trainer, says he has known Brewer for a long time and that he is an easy player to get along with.

"Brewer is a real competitor," said Haggert. "He gets all wrapped up in the game. He is a really good guy and nice to get along with. He doesn't give you any trouble."

In another week the Leafs will break camp and start a series of exhibition games. After meeting New York Rangers in Peterborough on Sept. 30 and in Toronto on Oct. 2, Toronto play games in Buffalo, Rochester and Kitchener before meeting Chicago Black Hawks in Toronto.

For the next 10 days, the Maple Leafs are on the road as they touch Chicago, New York, Quebec, Peterborough (Oct. 14 against Boston), London and Detroit before playing at home.

The regular NHL schedule starts Oct. 23—two weeks later than usual—and hockey for Brewer could last until the middle of May if the Leafs advance to the Stanley Cup finals.

"Hockey is a wonderful, interesting and artistic game," said Brewer. "It is a thrilling and a challenging game.

*"The satisfaction is great, not only financially. There
is the satisfaction of knowing you played a good game, you
made good passes and you scored a winning goal."*

The mile-long walk to the rink? That was one of
Imlach's rules, though there were mornings when the
players did their best to find an alternative just so long
as no one was watching. They might hitch a ride with
a friendly, starstruck local, or sometimes, they'd park
their own cars as close to the arena as they dared, then
try their best to look sweaty and tired when they walked
through the dressing room door.

The coach was also a firm believer in golf as exercise,
as a team builder, as a holistic few hours in the great,
albeit manicured, outdoors. Afternoons spent at the
Kawartha Golf and Country Club were every bit as
mandatory as mornings spent at the rink.

And those early nights? There was indeed an 11:15
curfew, and phone calls and bed checks were a familiar
part of the routine—with fines for those who were
caught breaking the rules. Early in camp, Brewer and
Bob Pulford found themselves busted down to early-
morning minor-league sessions after sleeping in—though
it was suggested that the Peterborough town hall clock,
which chimed every hour on the hour all through the
night, was interrupting the players' rest more than any
extracurricular activities.

But still, occasionally, during that long stretch cooped
up in the Empress Hotel, players would find a way to slip
out to one of the local watering holes, the local branch

of the Royal Canadian Legion, or a bar frequented by
the rock-and-roll musician Rompin' Ronnie Hawkins. All
fine just so long as Imlach, Clancy, or Joe Crozier didn't
find out, or any damage done wasn't too obvious at
practice the next morning.

"Punch and Clance would always be trying to catch
us," Bob Baun remembers. "We'd fall under the tables.
We'd do whatever. We were crazy as bedbugs. They'd do
whatever they thought they could do to try and nail us.
But that group of guys there were up before the birds."

Though Brewer painted himself as the happy worker for
the benefit of a reporter, he was in fact anything but. He
was a sensitive man, and Imlach's constant bullying had
worn him down and drained away much of his love of
the game. Many years later, Brewer described his feelings
this way:

"My damaged psyche—destroyed by Imlach—would
no longer allow me to accommodate playing hockey and
being a hockey player."

The lives of most professional athletes are so
completely devoted to their sport, to the exclusion of
other interests and pursuits, that there is rarely cause to
ask big, existential questions. Brewer, though, had already
begun to wonder whether there might not be more to
life, whether hockey really was his only destiny. Why
couldn't he do something else, or be something else?

He had considered walking away from the team
before, and had actually retired briefly in 1960 in a
dispute over $100 he believed he was owed in medical

expenses—Brewer said he was going to play football for McMaster University, but came back when the Leafs relented and paid him $200. In the end, no matter what his level of discontent, he had always fallen back into the routine of training camp and into his role.

Then, during an October 14 exhibition game against the Boston Bruins at the Peterborough Memorial Arena, Brewer experienced a kind of epiphany.

Here's how Imlach recalled it (with the help of Scott Young) in his book *Hockey Is a Battle*: "We were playing an exhibition game in Peterborough this particular night when the puck went into the corner and Johnny Bower yelled at Carl to get in there and get it out. All I could see from behind the bench was that Brewer went into the corner and shot it right out in front. Someone on the opposite team took a swipe at it and it almost hit Bower in the face. Then the puck went back in the corner, and damned if Brewer didn't go for it and shoot it out front again and once more Bower almost got creamed."

Imlach yelled at Brewer when he came back to the bench.

Brewer yelled, "To hell with it," and stormed off to the Leafs' dressing room at the end of the period.

During the break, Brewer and Bower continued to argue. One version of the story has Brewer throwing an orange at Bower and yelling at him, "Don't take your old-man frustrations out on me."

"I may be old but I'll be around this league longer than you will," was Bower's response.

In his book, Imlach says that he told Brewer, "If you don't want to play, stay in the room."

So Brewer did. As his teammates filed out and onto the ice for the third period, Brewer was changing into his street clothes. While they finished the game, he left the building—and left the Toronto Maple Leafs.

Back at the Empress Hotel, Brewer happened to run into Paul Rimstead, then a young reporter with *The Globe and Mail*—precisely the kind of good fortune that has led to many a scoop. Brewer told Rimstead that he was quitting hockey, that he was retiring, that he was finished with the Leafs and finished with the sport, and that he was going home.

Rimstead did his best to explain that decision to his readers, describing an athlete far more complex, more human, more vulnerable than the familiar bubblegum-card image.

"When Carl was dejected, or worrying, he'd prefer sitting with a stranger instead of a teammate on a trip—just to talk," Rimstead wrote. "He's a deep thinker and enjoyed discussing many subjects outside of hockey.

"Brewer suffered at his career in hockey for a long time. At one point, he was losing his hair in patches and had problems with a rash, supposedly caused by a nervous condition.

"He admits that he had second thoughts about showing up at training camp this season. Once before, he left the team during camp to contemplate his future. He felt at that time that he'd be happier as a high school teacher."

(This is how Brewer's friend and teammate Bob Baun remembers the situation today: "I knew when Carl had the head worms—that's what I called them. He was Dr. Jekyll and Mr. Hyde. When he decided what he was going to do, there was no turning him back. I was like a brother to him and we cared a lot about one another. He was so bright. That was probably his biggest problem— that he was too bright. For him to deal with Punch . . . he just didn't want any part of that.")

Of course, Imlach saw it a little differently.

"Carl is upset," he said. "He had a great three weeks, looked like he was going to have his best camp as a Leaf. Then he tailed off and nothing has gone right for him lately. I'm sure he'll settle down after a few days at home and will rejoin us in Toronto Monday."

Years later, when looking back on that tumultuous camp, Imlach added another character to the story—in his opinion, the true architect of Brewer's walkout.

"To my mind, Brewer would still be with the Leafs today if some of his influences outside the club had been different," he wrote in *Hockey Is a Battle*. "I'm talking now about Alan Eagleson, the lawyer for the Players Association. He got into hockey as the players' lawyer and he started trying to work a revolution. . . . One thing I do know is that he was very chummy with Brewer, who was a bit of a rebel himself. So you have two rebels talking together, bracing each other up, telling each other that they're great guys and Imlach is the bloody villain, and pretty soon something is going to happen."

(It is no small irony that, years later, Brewer became one of Eagleson's most dogged antagonists, leading the crusade that eventually landed the former union head in jail.)

Brewer's name would continue to come up as the Leafs' 1965 training camp played out, though he never returned to Peterborough. Four days after leaving camp, he officially announced his retirement at Maple Leaf Gardens.

"Hockey's a great game," he said, "but I've decided to retire for personal reasons. That's all I care to say."

There were rumours that Brewer planned to enter politics as Red Kelly had (his friend Eagleson was, at the time, a member of Ontario's provincial legislature), but he said that talk was premature. "I've already made one very big decision," he said. "I'd want a while before making the next one."

Imlach did his best to not sound worried about losing one of his best defencemen. As he was all too happy to point out, the big trade with Detroit in the off-season had already provided the perfect replacement: Marcel Pronovost.

"I have to be the luckiest guy in the world," Imlach said. "I gave up guys I didn't want for players I hoped I might be able to use. That's all. I had no inkling Brewer would quit."

Plus, looking a little farther down the road, the Leafs believed they already had a superstar in the making, a teenaged defenceman with the Toronto Marlboros named Jim McKenny.

"Although only 18, McKenny is the finest defensive prospect in the system," Ken McKee wrote in the *Toronto*

Star, "and the Leafs privately feel he's better than Oshawa's celebrated Bobby Orr."

The only question remaining was whether Brewer would participate in the upcoming NHL All-Star Game, in those days a contest between the reigning Stanley Cup champion and the best talent from the other five teams. It was played before the regular season began, with the proceeds going to the players' pension fund.

Brewer was scheduled to be part of the squad that would take on the Montreal Canadiens at the Forum. But now that he was retired and about to enroll at the University of Toronto, the decision of whether to play or not play wasn't quite so simple. No player could compete in the All-Star Game without being under contract— Bobby Hull's refusal to sign was threatening to keep him out—plus there were issues regarding liability should he be injured.

Brewer consulted his friend Eagleson, and they came up with a proposal.

"I'll play in the game, but that doesn't mean that I'm rescinding my decision to quit the Leafs," Brewer said. There were a couple of conditions attached, one of which was immediately misinterpreted.

"I asked two things: that Mr. [Stafford] Smythe make it plain to a network television audience that I had agreed to play this game only; and that I be guaranteed last season's salary, plus $2,000, in the event I suffered a serious injury—like a broken leg," Brewer said. "I couldn't understand the comment of League President Clarence

Campbell that I was asking for $2,000 to play in the All-Star Game. I didn't ask for a penny to play. All I asked for was some security in the event I was hurt."

Of course, Campbell's suggestion that Brewer was asking for money to play in a charity game caused a brief media furor, which the clarification only partially tamped down.

In the end, Brewer opted not to play. He said that he didn't want to confuse the fans as to his true intentions.

There were some, including Leaf owner Stafford Smythe, who thought that the real reason for Brewer's discontent was what was happening with his friend and teammate, Bob Baun. At age twenty-eight, the defenceman was one of the club's stalwarts, and had famously played on after breaking his ankle and scored the winning goal in overtime of game six of the 1964 Stanley Cup final against the Detroit Red Wings. The Leafs went on to win that Cup in game seven, only after which did Baun disclose his injury. In myth and lore, it became the tough-guy tale against which all other sports tough-guy tales are measured.

Unbeknownst to fans of the era, Baun had become one of the few hockey players to try and understand the business of the game, at least in terms of how it affected his own compensation. He entered contract negotiations prepared with numbers that highlighted his performance, and with as much information as he could glean about the salaries being paid to others. Quietly, teammates and even players from other teams had begun to seek his counsel before they went in to meet the general manager, looking for advice on how to get the best possible deal.

On the surface, Baun's dispute would have seemed like so many others, the kind of ritual training camp haggling that happened every year in the only professional sport in which players could participate in camp without having signed a contract. In 1965, he was one of several Leafs who were initially reluctant to accept what Imlach had offered, and his negotiations figured to follow a predictable course.

There would be a bit of grumbling both from the players and from Imlach, a bit of negotiation through the press, including the odd empty threat. Then, one by one, the players would make their way to Imlach's office and hash out a deal, each side claiming victory, which would allow them to go on living the dream of playing for a storied franchise in the National Hockey League.

But Baun's deeper discontent, his knowledge of the game's true economics and his willingness to fight for what he believed he deserved made this standoff different, in some ways a precursor to the player-management wars that were coming in all sports.

During the early days of camp, Baun seemed content to toe the party line and paint a happy picture, at least when speaking to a reporter.

"We have a much better attitude," he said. "Punch has been more relaxed, and despite the fact we have more good players than a year ago, the pressure hasn't been as great. Take the Big M, that trip to Europe last summer has done wonders for him, brought him right out of his shell. Last year he hardly said two words all training camp. Now he's taking part in conversations, holding his own in the verbal needling department, and look at the way he's moving on the ice. It's hard to explain why we should be working harder and enjoying it more. I guess last year we knew we had a chance to become the first Leaf team to win four straight Stanley Cups and the pressure cooked us. Now we're no longer champs, just guys trying to climb higher than fourth place. I'm convinced we'll play better."

But just a week after that story ran, and just before Brewer quit the team, Baun didn't show up for a team flight to Chicago, where the Leafs were set to play the Black Hawks in an exhibition game. Instead, he packed his bags, checked out of the Empress, and went home to Toronto. According to Smythe, that's what put Brewer over the edge.

"The Brewer incident grew out of the Baun incident," he said. "Brewer simply couldn't comprehend a situation such as Baun packing up and departing from training camp. Why, Baun is a guy with a blue maple leaf tattooed on each arm. The day Baun left camp, he warned me that Brewer was disturbed by what had happened. He also told me not to be shocked if Brewer left. So I must admit I wasn't surprised when it happened."

While Brewer was suffering through a larger crisis of desire and confidence, Baun's needs were pretty straightforward. He had asked Imlach for a $10,000-a-year raise. Imlach countered by offering $2,000 and showed no signs of budging.

"I was always holding out, but that was part of our game plan," Baun explained in an interview forty-eight years later. "We'd use that. I'd go in first, or Carl would go in first, or Al MacNeil before that—I'd send him in first. I'd go in and we'd go back and forth back and forth and just play Mickey Mouse with him, because we couldn't get any information out of the old guys. The old guys wouldn't give us the time of day. So we never knew what a good salary was."

Baun's walkout became the main training camp narrative in 1965. Nearly every day, one reporter or another would ask Imlach if there were any developments.

"No comment," Imlach barked. "Why don't you ask Baun?"

Then they'd call Baun at home.

"No comment," Baun said. "You're wasting your money. Why don't you ask Punch?"

Nature and sportswriting both abhor a vacuum, and so rumours began circulating. There was a story floating around that Baun would be traded, along with fellow malcontent Eddie Shack, to the New York Rangers in return for Bob Nevin and Vic Hadfield, though of course the deal never materialized.

There were rumbles about a larger walkout, a mutiny against Imlach by Baun's unsigned teammates.

"Don't be surprised," columnist Red Burnett wrote in the *Toronto Star,* "if a couple more join Baun on the sidelines before the season opens on Oct. 23. No one is talking for the record, but all make it known that they intend to be very militant in any further salary negotiations with Imlach."

Outside of Toronto, the rest of the hockey world was taking notice. When the Leafs played Chicago in an exhibition game, Bobby Hull—still embroiled in his own contract dispute with the team—couldn't help rubbing it in.

"We started taking liberties when we realized Baun wasn't in town," he said. "When he's around, that right side is like an obstacle course. He seldom lets you get set for a real good shot. But I hope he settles his salary problems. The league needs guys like him."

But the game's greatest icon wasn't going to be part of any revolution. When the Leafs played the Detroit Red Wings in an exhibition game, Gordie Howe was asked about the notion that players ought to share salary information in order to help them secure a fair wage in negotiation.

"It took me 20 years to get where I am on the salary scale," Howe said. "All I'll tell them is that my salary is satisfactory and I'm happy. I signed quite a while ago and if I decide to play next season, it will be at the same salary."

(That would not be the last time that Howe and Baun would intersect. In what is arguably the most famous passage from their groundbreaking 1991 book *Net Worth,* David Cruise and Alison Griffiths recreated a conversation between Baun and Howe after the defenceman joined the Wings in 1968. Howe had always been led to believe by the Wings' general manager, Jack Adams, that he was the highest-paid player in the league. Every year, Adams would hand Howe a contract with a blank space where the salary figure was supposed to go, and tell Howe to fill in whatever he thought he was worth. Howe would dutifully give himself a $1,000 raise. In his rookie year, when the Wings were disingenuously pleading poverty, he accepted a new hockey jacket as a signing bonus. "Don't ever divulge what you're making," Adams told Howe. "It would make the other players jealous." It was only when his new teammate Baun informed him that he was earning $67,000–which was $22,000 more than Howe–that the veteran right wing understood his loyalty had been used against him and he'd been played for a patsy all those years.)

As training camp continued, with Baun occasionally dropping in to talk contract with Imlach before once again heading home, the Leafs' ownership began to get nervous. But instead of blaming the player, Stafford Smythe–in a conversation with *Toronto Star* columnist Milt Dunnell–abandoned the hard-line stance he had taken earlier in the same training camp and put responsibility for the impasse at Imlach's feet.

"My part of the operation is to sell tickets," Smythe said. "I also sell television of hockey. How do we justify ourselves to the public if we don't show them Brewer, Baun, Pulford, Keon? Another thing: We've built up our All-Star game and so what happens? We're making a mockery of it if we don't show the fans the players I have mentioned. As I understand it, Bobby Hull may not be in it, either. There's an owners' meeting tomorrow and

hell will be popping. Usually, I'm the one under the gun. This time, I'll have company. . . .

"Let me say this. There is no such thing as a salary budget. Punch has the authority to sign the players for what he thinks they're worth. But it is up to him to sign the players. His job depends on it."

Three days before the season opener, Baun and Imlach finally hashed out a deal, a one-year contract that gave Baun an $8,000 raise, pushing his salary past $20,000. "I went for two years once," Baun explained. "Never again. You lose the chance to cash in on a good year, and even if you have a bad one, this organization never asks you to take a cut. So you can't gain anything."

Soon after, Baun would sit down and talk to Bob Woolf, who was to become one of the first player agents. The world of sport was changing, and Baun would be at the cutting edge.

The remaining holdouts fell into place once Baun's contract was signed, the last of them finalizing their deals at Maple Leaf Gardens, sitting in the arena's coffee shop while King Clancy shuttled back and forth to Imlach's office with offers and counteroffers. Bob Pulford, a future general manager, was, as always, the last to sign on the dotted line.

"We negotiated on a United Nations level," Dave Keon quipped, pulling out a contemporary political reference to Nikita Krushchev, "but no one pounded the desk with his shoe."

·

With that final bit of housekeeping completed, Punch Imlach announced his roster for the 1965–66 season.

In goal, he had Johnny Bower, who would start the season opener against the Chicago Black Hawks, and Terry Sawchuk, who would start the next night against Detroit. On defence, the pairings would be Bob Baun and Marcel Pronovost, Tim Horton and Allan Stanley, with Kent Douglas as a spare. The forward lines had Dave Keon between Larry Jeffrey and Ron Ellis; Red Kelly centring Frank Mahovlich and Jim Pappin; and Bob Pulford with wingers Orland Kurtenbach and team captain George Armstrong. Brit Selby, the only rookie to make the squad, and Larry Joyal were the extra forwards.

At the end of Red Burnett's final training camp column, there were a couple of notes that tied up loose ends.

"Centre Mike Walton and defenceman Don Cherry have been assigned to Tulsa by the Leafs," it said in the fine print. And: "Terry Sawchuk is still looking for accommodations. He needs at least two bedrooms. Interested parties are asked to contact Stan Obodiac at the Gardens, EM. 8-1641."

On October 23, the Toronto Maple Leafs began the season against the Chicago Black Hawks, their thirty-fifth home opener at Maple Leaf Gardens. Fans at the Carlton Street arena immediately noticed something different. Absent was the familiar voice of Red Barber, who had been the arena's public address announcer since it opened in 1931. Barber had retired during the summer. His replacement was a thirty-one-year-old with a distinctive nasal twang to his voice by the name of Paul Morris.

During the first intermission, Imlach sat down for an interview with *Hockey Night in Canada*'s Ward Cornell to discuss what lay ahead. The travails of training camp and the difficult season past didn't seem to have shaken his confidence in the least.

"We only loaned the Cup to the Canadiens for a year," he said. "We'll try to get it back this year."

The Leafs lost the game 4–0. Bobby Hull, having settled his contract issues with the Hawks, scored a hat trick. After his third goal, the Toronto crowd gave him a standing ovation, a comment on both the Golden Jet's hockey genius and the home team's ineptitude.

Among those watching the game was Bing Crosby. The word was that, with expansion coming, he wanted to put money into a team in San Francisco.

The next night, the Maple Leafs lost again, 3–0 in Detroit, and their fans were already wondering whether all of the brave, optimistic talk during training camp was merely empty rhetoric, whether this wasn't simply an old team in decline, whether Imlach had permanently lost his touch.

POSTSCRIPT

After announcing his retirement in 1965, Carl Brewer didn't return to the Maple Leafs that year, but he certainly wasn't done with hockey, or with the club, though his ambivalence about the game—and especially the business of the game—became a recurring theme in his life.

The following year, Brewer decided that he wanted to return to the ice and play for Canada's national team. To do so, though, would require regaining his amateur status, and since Brewer was technically a retired member of the Toronto Maple Leafs, that would require Imlach's approval, which Imlach was reluctant to grant, along with the other teams agreeing to waive him out of the league. Eventually, Brewer won that battle and played a year with the Nats, winning a bronze medal at the 1967 World Championships, not long before Canada opted out of international competition because its best weren't allowed to play.

In March of 1968, Brewer returned to professional hockey with the Muskegon Mohawks of the International Hockey League, where he served as player/coach—and, in addition to his salary, received a cut of the gate. The next season, he headed for Europe, where he was player/coach of HIFK Helsinki and took university courses. It was during that season overseas that Brewer accepted an offer to skate with CSKA Moscow, the Soviet Red Army team coached by Anatoli Tarasov that contained the nucleus of the powerful national side of the USSR. Tarasov was already an admirer of Brewer's from his time in the NHL

and was trying to enhance his understanding of Canadian pros, knowing that a showdown between them and the Big Red Machine was inevitable.

Imlach threw in Brewer's playing rights as part of what would become arguably the biggest trade in the history of the Maple Leafs. From the Detroit Red Wings, Toronto received a complete forward line—Norm Ullman, Paul Henderson, and Floyd Smith—in return for Frank Mahovlich, Pete Stemkowski, Garry Unger, and the right to sign Brewer. With Mahovlich and Baun—by then a Red Wing—doing their best to persuade him, Brewer returned to the NHL with the Wings for the 1969–70 season. He didn't miss a beat, playing so well he made the second all-star team before announcing his retirement—again.

Brewer came back once more, in time to play the following two years with the St. Louis Blues—and then retired. He signed with the Toronto Toros of the World Hockey Association, where he played a single season in 1973–74, and then once again announced that he was finished with professional hockey.

No one would have predicted Brewer's *final* final go-round, or the impetus for it. At age forty-one, following six years away from the game, he was persuaded to make one more comeback by a desperate Imlach, who had returned to the Leafs as general manager in what would be a disastrous encore with the franchise in 1979.

It was one of the darkest eras in Maple Leafs history. When Lanny McDonald was traded away, captain Darryl Sittler removed the *C* from his jersey in protest. Brewer's arrival certainly didn't make things any better.

But he set all of his old battles and grievances with Imlach aside because he said that he wanted to die a Maple Leaf, and it didn't hurt that Imlach handed him a pro-rated $125,000 contract to return to the team. The other players immediately decided that Brewer was Imlach's spy in the dressing room and refused to pass him the puck, even in practice. Though Brewer played reasonably well, the experiment ended after twenty games, and his playing career was finally over, for real.

Still to come was his crusade to win retired NHL players their rightful pension benefits, which put Eagleson square in his sights.

Brewer died in 2001.

Eddie Shack managed to get himself back into Imlach's good books, and after eight games with the Rochester Americans, he was recalled and spent the rest of the season with the Maple Leafs, putting up some of the best numbers of his professional career, playing with his characteristic wild abandon. It was during the 1965–66 season that Shack gained a kind of immortality. Noting how the fans at the Gardens reacted every time Shack touched the puck, hockey broadcaster Brian McFarlane had a bright idea. He penned the lyrics to a novelty song extolling Shack's unusual virtues, and then approached a group of teenaged musicians he'd heard entertaining one night at the Toronto Pressmen's Club. The band—Douglas Rankine and the Secrets—had just recorded their first single, but that would be immediately forgotten in the wake of what was to come. Anyone of a certain age

has the lyrics embedded in memory, whether they want them there or not.

> *Clear the track*
> *Here comes Shack*
> *He knocks 'em down and he gives them a whack*
> *He can score goals*
> *He's found the knack*
> *Eddie, Eddie Shack*
>
> *They call him the great entertainer*
> *But our boy Eddie's no clown*
> *It couldn't be made any plainer*
> *It's great to have Eddie in town*
>
> *He started the year in the minors*
> *And almost gave up the game*
> *But boom, he's back with the big club*
> *And the Leafs haven't quite been the same*
>
> *It's great to see him on right wing*
> *Or is it the left wing he plays?*
> *Maybe it's both at the same time*
> *He skates all over the place*
>
> *Someday in the dim distant future*
> *When they honour the greats of the game*
> *They'll hang up his skates and his sweater*
> *In our hockey hall of fame*

·

The song, "(Clear the Track) Here Comes Shack" (the almost never-heard B-side was called "Warming the Bench"), was a hit, eventually spending two weeks at the top of the CHUM radio charts. "We didn't know it was going to be released as a single and played across the entire country," Rankine said in an interview years later. "Once it was released, we thought (or hoped) it would just disappear into the night and nobody would care about it. As fate would have it, it didn't disappear. For some reason, people loved it." In order to try and escape the song, the band was renamed Quiet Jungle, and it released another, very different record. But when they went on the road, the crowd inevitably called for "Clear the Track."

For his part, Shack complained because he didn't receive any royalties from the single, though he would reap the benefits of that '65–66 season for years, becoming a full-fledged local celebrity who appeared in television commercials long after he had retired from hockey in 1975, following stops in Boston, Los Angeles, Buffalo, Pittsburgh, and a final encore in Toronto.

Brit Selby was the only one of the young players in camp to enjoy immediate NHL success, making the Leafs and sticking with the club for the entire '65–66 season, capping the year by winning the Calder Memorial Trophy as the NHL's top rookie. That would turn out to be the peak of his pro career. He was demoted to the minors the next season, then claimed by the Philadelphia Flyers in the expansion draft, returned to the Leafs, was traded to St. Louis, and eventually bounced around the World Hockey Association before leaving hockey for a career as a school teacher.

Brian Conacher played only two games with the Leafs in 1965–66, spending the rest of the season as a very productive member of their AHL farm team, the Rochester Americans. He made the big club the following season, and in all played 155 games in the NHL with the Leafs and the Detroit Red Wings, another 69 in the WHA, and he played a second stint with the Canadian National Team. While he may not have lived up to the expectations attached to his famous last name, Conacher later enjoyed a successful career in and around hockey, managing both Copps Coliseum and Maple Leaf Gardens. In 1972, he served as the colour commentator, working beside Foster Hewitt, on the iconic television broadcast of the Summit Series.

After being sent down to Rochester in 1965, Mike Walton responded by being named the AHL's rookie of the year and was a key part of the Americans team that won the 1966 Calder Cup. He finally made the Leafs midway through the following season, and the year after that was the team's leading scorer. But his clashes with Imlach continued, and his exit became inevitable. In February 1971, Walton was traded to the defending Stanley Cup champion Boston Bruins, where he was part of a championship team the following season. His later hockey travels would take him to the Minnesota Fighting Saints of the WHA (where he won a league scoring title), the Vancouver Canucks, the St. Louis Blues, and the

Chicago Black Hawks, before a final professional season in Germany in 1980.

A year later, when the Leafs returned to Peterborough for training camp, Bob Baun's already tense relationship with Imlach took a turn for the worse. Walking through the halls of the Empress Hotel, the coach spotted a group of young Leafs players lined up outside the door to Baun's room, waiting their turn to get advice on the art of contract negotiation. He didn't much like that, and Baun paid the price. By season's end, even as the franchise returned to glory, Baun found himself nailed to the bench. He skipped out on the dressing room Stanley Cup celebrations in 1967, took a pass on the victory parade, and then was left unprotected in the expansion draft, where he was the first position player claimed by the Oakland Seals.

One season in California was enough for Baun. He asked to be traded back to an Original Six team, and wound up in Detroit, where he played a little more than two seasons, was eventually reunited with his old teammates Frank Mahovlich and Carl Brewer, and had his famous, eye-opening chat with Gordie Howe.

Baun finished his NHL career as a Leaf between 1970 and 1973, then spent a single season as the coach of the WHA Toronto Toros before leaving the game behind.

Eventually, he was forgiving enough to let bygones be bygones.

"Punch and I kissed and made up and became dear friends later on," Baun told the *Toronto Star* in 2012. "I was actually waiting for Punch for lunch on the day that he died (December 1, 1987). We'd meet once a month, have a nice lunch together and reminisce about the old times and how I caused him a lot of heartache. It was all good fun."

Those undercurrents that Punch Imlach was feeling in 1965—players thinking independently, agents being hired, unions being formed—would only get stronger as the 1960s rolled on. The coach and general manager was slow to adapt. On the ice, he stuck with his old guys because he knew them and trusted them, and that intransigence, whatever the short-term reward, would mortally wound the Toronto franchise in a rapidly changing sport and a rapidly changing business. By 1969, when the Leafs fired Imlach following a first-round playoff loss to Bobby Orr and the Boston Bruins, he seemed a man out of the past, a relic of a bygone era.

That belief, however, didn't extend to the owners of the Buffalo Sabres, one of two franchises (along with the Vancouver Canucks) added during a second round of NHL expansion in 1970. They hired Imlach to get their team off the ground, to become its first coach and general manager, and he did a splendid job of that, winning the spin of a wheel for the right to draft Gilbert Perreault first overall and putting together a team that was playing in the Stanley Cup final in just its fifth season of existence.

In Buffalo, Imlach continued his pattern of feuding with star players—most notably, Jim Schoenfeld—and was finally shown the door in 1978, which most assumed would mark his swan song in the NHL.

But they hadn't taken into account the eccentricities of Harold Ballard, who had seized full control of the Leafs in 1972 following the death of his partner, Stafford Smythe.

Coming off the 1978–79 season, the Leafs were hardly in dire straits; the team, led by Darryl Sittler and Lanny McDonald, had beaten the New York Islanders in the Stanley Cup quarter-finals in 1978, and though the following season marked an 11-point decline in the standings the core remained solid. Ballard, though, believed otherwise, and felt Imlach would be just the tonic, hiring him in the summer of 1979 as coach and general manager.

At the press conference announcing his return, Imlach threw down the gauntlet, declaring that there were only "five or six" decent players on the entire squad, and immediately the battle began.

Imlach tried to roll back the clock to a time when coaches and general managers were feared. He ordered the players into jackets and ties. He picked a fight over their participation in a television feature called "Showdown," a skills competition that aired between periods on *Hockey Night in Canada* and put a few extra bucks in the players' pockets.

When that didn't work, when the players balked, when they (and their agents) began whispering behind his back, Imlach began the process of blowing up a team that he believed was complacent and too dominated by Sittler (who, in Imlach's mind, was in turn being manipulated by his old nemesis Eagleson). Leafs fans of a certain vintage, sadly, remember it well: the Lanny McDonald and Tiger Williams trades, Sittler stripping the captain's *C* from the front of his uniform, Brewer's short comeback, a full dressing-room insurrection, with unnamed players filling the local newspapers with juicy details, and finally Imlach's ignominious exit—after suffering a heart attack, he was effectively fired without Ballard telling him he had been dismissed. He arrived at the Gardens one day to find that his parking space had been assigned to someone else.

A proud franchise seemed to have reached its nadir, though with Ballard's sad and destructive final years to come, and later revelations of child sexual abuse inside Maple Leaf Gardens, it actually still had a distance to fall.

Imlach was wrong in that between-periods interview when he said the 1965–66 Toronto Maple Leafs had just loaned out the Stanley Cup to the Habs for a year. They finished the season with a respectable, winning record, in third place, but then were swept in the semifinals by the eventual champions, once more the Montreal Canadiens.

The next fall, the team assembled once again in Peterborough. By the time the Leafs broke camp, it was clear that the roster would remain largely unchanged, that an old team was now starting to look like an ancient one, and few gave them any chance to contend in what would be the final season before NHL expansion.

In the spring of 1967, the Toronto Maple Leafs won the Stanley Cup, defeating the Canadiens in six games.

They have not won it since. ❧

A group of local women outside the Empress Hotel.

HIT THE TOWN

The front entrance of the Empress Hotel. The players remember the hotel as a decent place to stay. When he saw this picture, Ron Ellis joked that the women must have been Bob Baun's girlfriends.

Minor-league players arriving at the Leafs' training camp
headquarters, the Empress Hotel, in downtown Peterborough.

View of the radio station next to the Empress Hotel—players were required to do some air time on the station—in part because the owner of the station was a friend of Punch Imlach.

An iconic Woolworth's sign across the street
from the Empress Hotel.

Left: The marquee of the Empress Hotel.

A Peterborough landmark—the town clock.

Parker passed the boxes to Patchett, and Patchett pitched them into the inferno, one after another, until a note on a file folder caught his eye: LEAFS 1965. Inside were photographic negatives and contact sheets.

"What are these?" Patchett asked.

Parker began to tell him a story.

"I think we'd better keep them," Patchett said, not yet fully understanding just what it was that he had preserved.

Downtown Peterborough, Ontario, September 1965.

A parking lot in downtown Peterborough. That's what cars looked like in the 1960s.

The mile-long walk to the rink? That was one of Imlach's rules, though there were mornings when the players did their best to find an alternative just so long as no one was watching.

Players, including Wayne Mosdell (centre), leaving the Empress Hotel coffee shop.

The lobby of the Empress Hotel. Don't forget to try
the chicken croquettes.

Right: Bob Pulford converses with a Leafs' farmhand as Tulsa
manager Ray "The Carp" Miron listens in.

At the hotel coffee shop Leafs prospects pour over the
latest news from camp.

We hope that you have enjoyed the summer and that you will attend Camp with the attitude that now we are Stanley Cup holders we will show everybody that we deserve it and intend to keep it.

George "Punch" Imlach, in a letter to Jim Pappin on August 2, 1962

The same group, doing their best not to pay attention to photographer Lewis Parker.

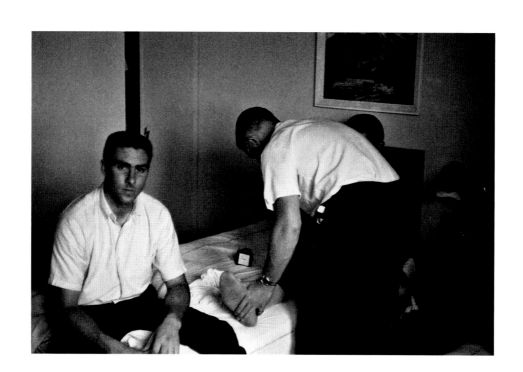

Whatever the doctor is telling this Leafs farmhand, it draws a laugh from "Cowboy" Bill Flett.

Left: An unidentified Leafs prospect looks into the camera as a doctor examines Bill Flett's ankle.

Orland Kurtenbach and Bill Smith kill time in one of the hotel rooms.

Bob Pulford grabbing forty winks in his hotel room. The players were up early in the morning and had curfews at night—which they regularly tried to break.

The Leafs stayed two to a room at the Empress.

PETERBOROUG
MEMORIAL
COMMUNITY
CENTRE
SUPERCAR BINGO
FRI SEPT 24
ROCHESTER VS
MAPLE LEAFS SAT
PEPSI
FISH & CHIPS
COIN WASH
Player's

Carl Brewer, in his street clothes, arriving for practice.

Last winter, Mahovlich came unstrung

emotionally and missed five weeks of the

season. By the time he returned, the Leafs

were sagging, objects of scorn and abuse in

the Gardens.

Dick Beddoes, *The Globe and Mail*, September 21, 1965

The Big M, Frank Mahovlich, arrives for practice.

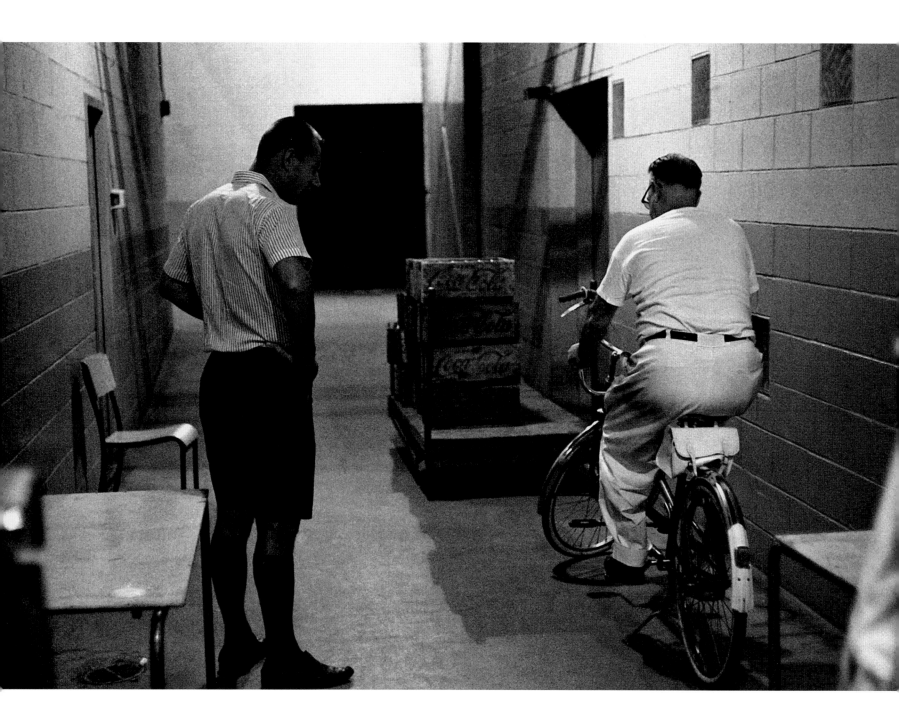

"I was mad, upset and confused (when I walked out). Let's face it, playing hockey is a nice way to make your living."

Eddie Shack

Eddie "The Entertainer" Shack tells Tommy Naylor how to ride the bike. Shack was bound for the minors, but by the end of the season would be a folk hero back in Toronto while "Clear the Track" climbed the charts.

Jim Pappin (front) and Bob Baun on the tandem bike. Baun brought his wife's bicycle to camp so he could get around Imlach's rule that players had to walk to the rink every morning.

HIT THE ICE

Carl Brewer is in the foreground as the Leafs stretch before practice.

Carl Brewer, stretching. He was haunted by doubts about whether he wanted to continue playing hockey.

Toe touching. That's Bob Pulford in front, who would go on to have the best season of his sixteen–year NHL career.

Left: Training camp pushups. Being a goalie meant doing them while wearing your pads.

Most players drank and smoked during the summer months, just as they did during the season. Naturally, they tended to put on a little weight and soften up around the edges.

Jim Pappin (far right), who was one of Imlach's favourite targets for criticism. After a bad loss, he was regularly threatened with demotion to the Leafs' farm team in Rochester.

Bob Pulford stickhandling across the blue line.

Carl Brewer (centre) and fellow Leafs during a skating drill.

Clancy remembered what a Maple Leafs training camp was like in the old days. His first was in 1930, in Parry Sound, where Conn Smythe brought twelve of his players to chop wood, exercise, take long walks, and sweat off their summer fat.

Watching practice, and having a smoke.

Below: Watching practice along the rail.

Players gather along the glass to watch a practice session.
That's Gary "Axe" Smith in goal.

The coach acknowledged that right wing, behind Ellis and Jim Pappin, might be a trouble spot and that he might consider moving defenceman Tim Horton there, as he had when injuries thinned the roster during the previous season.

Tim Horton and Nick Harbaruk.

A scrimmage during practice viewed through the
wire mesh behind the net.

Locals and a few members of the Leafs front office mingle
while watching practice.

A lone spectator, right, at practice.

There was no Zamboni at the Peterborough arena, so the Leafs had to bring in their own from Maple Leaf Gardens.

Above: Minor leaguers practice beneath the Union Jack, the red maple leaf—which had become Canada's new national flag earlier that year—and artist David Bierk's locally famous portrait of Queen Elizabeth II.

Right: That's Don Cherry on the left. The goalie is Bob Perreault. Darryl Sly is behind him and Pete Stemkowski is behind the net. The Leafs' minor-leaguers often had to make do with hand-me-down equipment.

That's the ageless Johnny Bower in net.

Imlach watches practice with Dick Beddoes, who has his
notebook at the ready.

In the stands, Punch Imlach catches up on the news.

In goal, [Punch Imlach] had Johnny Bower, who would start the season opener against the Chicago Black Hawks, and Terry Sawchuk, who would start the next night against Detroit.

Terry Sawchuk retrieves the puck while Leafs brass, including King Clancy (hand on chin) and Punch Imlach, look on.

Leafs' captain George Armstrong shooting on Terry Sawchuk during a scrimmage.

On the bench, a Leafs hopeful seems deep in thought.

A contemplative Carl Brewer sitting on the bench. Not long after this picture was taken, he would walk out of camp and announce his retirement from hockey.

By the fall of 1965, cracks were starting to appear in the old power structure. Plans were underway for the NHL to undertake the most ambitious expansion in the history of professional sport, doubling in size from six to twelve franchises all at once in the 1967–68 season, and taking the northern game into exotic southern climes in the United States.

An unidentified Rochester American player takes a break during practice. The Leafs' AHL farm team was stacked with veterans who were excited about reports of the upcoming NHL expansion.

Bob Pulford (foreground) and Larry Regan watching
intently from the bench.

Carl Brewer, whose retirement would become the biggest story
in training camp, lies exhausted on bench. Bob Pulford and
Larry Regan watch the ice.

Left: Players change lines; Bob Pulford is sitting on the bench
wearing a white singlet.

Eddie Joyal, one of the new arrivals from Detroit.

"You should hear my guys," Imlach told a group of reporters. "They say they're the best. You'd have thought we won the league and the Stanley Cup instead of finishing out in the first round last season. All of them had great years. I can't figure out how we lost if they all played that well."

Dick Beddoes, *The Globe and Mail* in hand, talks to radio newsman Joe Morgan.

HIT THE LOCKER ROOM

The Leafs dressing room in the Peterborough arena. It was small and it wasn't glamorous.

Left to right: Joe Sgro; Dick Beddoes taking notes; an arena worker; and Joe Morgan, the sports director of Foster Hewitt's radio station, CKFH.

Joe Sgro, who later became the Leafs' trainer, worked for
Toronto's Tulsa farm team during the 1965 camp.

The forward lines had Dave Keon between Larry Jeffrey and Ron Ellis; Red Kelly centring Frank Mahovlich and Jim Pappin; and Bob Pulford with wingers Orland Kurtenbach and team captain George Armstrong.

Joe Morgan talks to Leafs trainer Bob Haggert as *Globe and Mail* reporter Dick Beddoes and Frank Mahovlich listen in. Orland Kurtenbach concentrates on fixing his stick.

Orland Kurtenbach puts on his gear while Joe Morgan has a smoke
and the *Globe*'s Dick Beddoes tidies up.

Hard rock Orland Kurtenbach laces up his skates. Dick Beddoes and Bob Haggert are in the background.

The medical table. Note the handwritten
sign: "Weigh In Every Day."

Baun's walkout became the main training camp narrative in 1965. Nearly every day, one reporter or another would ask Imlach if there were any developments.

"No comment," Imlach barked. "Why don't you ask Baun?"

Then they'd call Baun at home.

"No comment," Baun said. "You're wasting your money. Why don't you ask Punch?"

Dick Beddoes, never without his trademark hat, shares a laugh with Leaf defenceman Bob Baun.

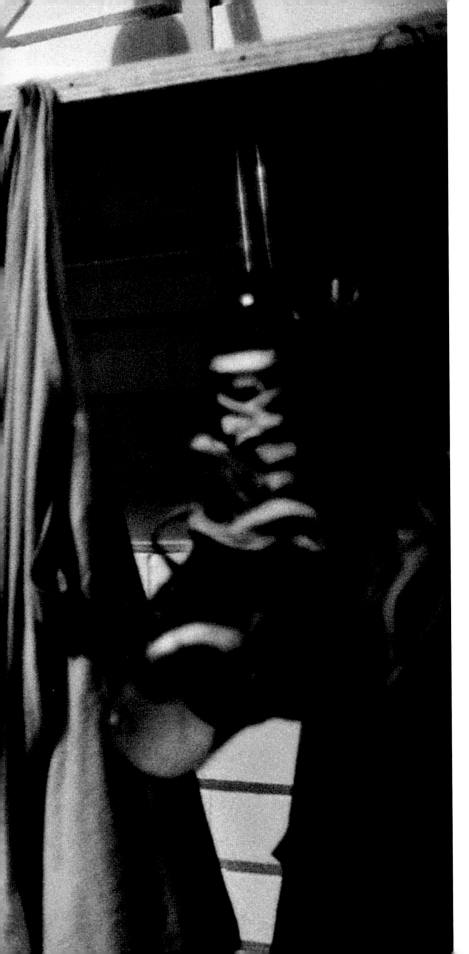

Skates on improvised hangers beside a Toronto
Maple Leafs baseball cap.

Tommy Naylor trying to fix Brewer's skate—the Leafs had one of
the best "skate people" on their staff.

The Leafs' equipment manager Tommy Naylor, who is given credit
for inventing the skate guard, among other safety innovations.

The skate-sharpening room. Note the cramped quarters.

Tommy Naylor retrieves a sweater from the ceiling while
Carl Brewer looks on, attaching his socks to his garters.

Long johns hung up to dry.

Every day since training started September 18, Brewer's thoughts have been on hockey. The day starts at 6:15 a.m. and it may not end until 11:15 p.m. – sometimes earlier. In those 17 hours or less, Brewer will have gone through a couple of hockey practices, a game of golf and an evening of relaxation before lights out at 11:15 p.m. at the Empress Hotel.

Peterborough Examiner profile on Carl Brewer, September 25, 1965

Carl Brewer putting on the last of his equipment before practice.

Bob Pulford ties his skates while former Marlboro Jack
Chipchase looks on. Chipchase played that season with the
Leafs' Tulsa farm team.

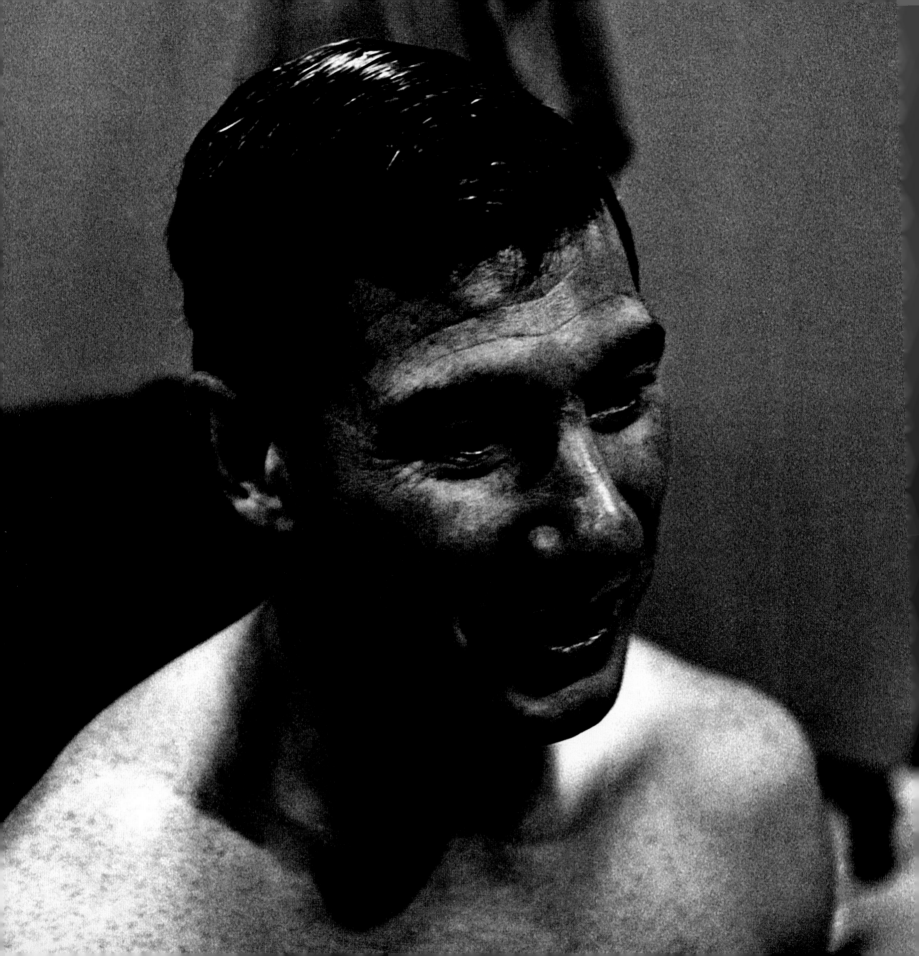

"My part of the operation is to sell tickets,"
Smythe said. "I also sell television of hockey.
How do we justify ourselves to the public if we
don't show them Brewer, Baun, Pulford, Keon?"

Bob Pulford.

Young Pete Stemkowski, hoping to stick with the Maple Leafs in what will be his second year as a pro. He went on to play fifty-six games for the Leafs that season.

The stick rack. They're all wood, the blades are all straight, and they're all made by CCM.

Frank Mahovlich, looking happy and relaxed. He had suffered
a nervous breakdown the season before, and had just
returned from a two-and-half-month vacation in Europe. That's
Red Kelly beside him.

161

Leafs' dressing room. On a hot September day the fan would have provided the only relief.

Punch Imlach gets ready to enjoy an ice cream cone, while an
arena worker looks on.

Second-year pro Ron Ellis was coming off summer knee surgery.
The season before, he'd scored twenty-three goals as a rookie.

Ron Ellis was recovering from midsummer knee surgery, following a terrific rookie campaign in 1964–65 during which he had scored twenty-three goals.

Twenty-year-old Ron Ellis checks out the knee that was surgically repaired over the summer.

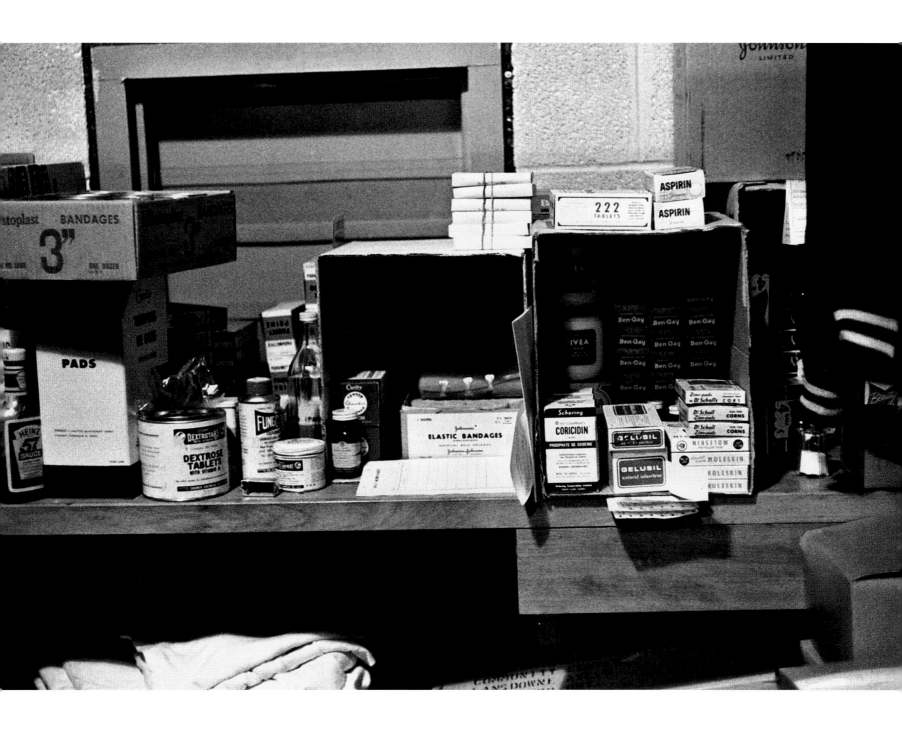

The team's medical supplies were basic. For some reason, they also include a bottle of steak sauce.

Five Hall of Famers—Allan Stanley (taping his stick), Francis "King" Clancy, Tim Horton, Marcel Pronovost, and Terry Sawchuk.

The tools of the goaltender's trade in an era when most didn't wear a mask.

Two old pros and former rivals, now teammates: Marcel Pronovost (left) and Johnny Bower (right).

Veteran defenceman Marcel Pronovost checks out his skates at
his first training camp as a Maple Leaf following the big off-season
trade that brought him from Detroit.

A Coke machine—in an era before energy drinks, having a pop
after practice was the norm.

Future Leafs captain Dave Keon walks towards the dressing room with trainer Bob Haggert (left) and a reporter.